An Introduction to
Ice Fishing

Frank R. Richards

Copyright © 2014 Frank R. Richards
All rights reserved.

ISBN: 1499329741
ISBN-13: 9781499329742
Library of Congress Control Number: 2014908406
CreateSpace Independent Publishing Platform
North Charleston, South Carolina

INTRODUCTION

I moved to Maine in the mid-1980s to start a new job. When that first winter arrived, one of my coworkers invited me to go ice fishing with him and his friends. I accepted, not knowing what to expect. Previously, I had been living in Iowa. I'd never tried fishing out on the ice before, although I'd fished on open water since I was a child.

That same afternoon he took me to a sporting goods store, where I bought basic equipment, such as a scoop, a minnow bucket, and tip-ups—items I would soon learn how to use. The tip-up was particularly interesting, an ingenious device that put a flag in the air when a fish pulled on a minnow suspended in the water below the ice.

The next Saturday at 4:00 a.m., I met my friend and two of his buddies in a parking lot, and together we headed out. Our destination was a large lake named—I kid you not—Moosehead Lake, a three-hour drive away. After we arrived and had breakfast, we were ready to set up and start fishing.

The area was beautiful. A rocky, cliff-like mountain rose directly from the water and extended several hundred feet up into the sky. The shoreline was forested, lined with fir trees.

My hosts had rented an ice shack with a small wood stove from a well-known, local sporting camp. The fishing instructions they provided me were simple. They advised putting my traps (their term for tip-ups) in a line, where I could see them from a window. They also suggested setting the bait about a foot off the bottom of the lake. Then they made a fire in the stove and broke out the beer, except one of them who preferred to drink wine.

The techniques they employed may not have been at the cutting edge of innovation. However, they were doing a lot of things right. We were protected from the cold, enjoying each other's company, and fishing in a good area. Very importantly, my hosts appreciated one of the more sublime aspects of ice fishing—the joy of the experience as well as anybody.

Not much later, a flag on one of my traps went up. We walked over to the hole and watched the line being pulled off the tip-up's reel a few inches under the water. Obviously, a good fish was on the other end. I grabbed the line to set the hook and slowly hauled in the first lake trout of my fishing career.

Later that afternoon, I caught another lake trout and a decent-sized landlocked salmon. I thought ice fishing was great! I couldn't wait to go out and do it again. Thirty years later, I wrote this book, *An Introduction to Ice Fishing,* to provide beginners with helpful hints and advice. It is my hope that this book will save readers a lot of trial and error.

Let me start by saying that ice fishing is really fun. An uninitiated observer may not see the entertainment in running around out in the middle of a frozen lake, heavily dressed. In reality, those who participate in this sport are usually feeling quite comfortable, having a good time, and catching fish.

Almost everyone will tell you that they just plain enjoy being out on the ice. There is something about the simplified, quasi-Arctic landscape that is peaceful and relaxing. At the same time, the experience can be highly social. There always seems to be something interesting to talk about while sitting around together, waiting for flags.

Ice fishing is also well-suited for small children. They enjoy being out on the ice. There is plenty of space for them to move around, and they like chasing flags. If you catch a few small fish and throw them a short distance away, they often attract birds—eagles, if you are lucky. Small children (as well as adults) are fascinated by watching them.

The pleasures of ice fishing are likely much the same today as they were for our parents and grandparents. Fortunately, clothing nowadays is lighter and more functional than in the past; the gear is more convenient. Still, knowing how to dress, organize, and transport a fair amount of equipment to the fishing grounds is essential to enjoying the enterprise. It takes a while to develop a system you like, but it is worth your time to think through those elements.

Also vital is your method for locating and catching fish. You will want to learn how to use depth maps to find good fishing places. This is a critical skill—even on good lakes, you probably won't catch much if you are not fishing at a suitable location.

Another important factor to appreciate is how oxygen levels and water temperatures change as the season progresses. In many lakes the oxygen in the water becomes too depleted under the ice for fish to be active, especially on relatively shallow lakes with clay bottoms.

Finally, I recommend spending a lot of time on water that is close to home. It is much easier to go fishing if you only need to travel a half hour or so from your residence. Over the long term, I also think you end up doing better because you are spending more time fishing than driving.

I suspect that some of you have been ice fishing and know how much fun it is. I hope you learn a few things from this book that will help you have a higher quality experience.

For readers who may have had no previous exposure, I'd like to encourage you to give it a try. I bet you won't regret it.

GENERAL PRINCIPLES

Fish feed aggressively during the late fall. They actively move around in search of prey, trying to build reserves for the lean winter months ahead. They will readily feed on any forage available.

Nearly all ice anglers will tell you that the action is best right after the ice forms. That is because oxygen levels are high at that time, and the water temperature is close to uniform throughout the lake. Fish continue to feed vigorously, extending that late fall "chow down" as long as they can.

After the ice has set in, it becomes too dark below for much photosynthesis to occur. It is no longer possible for wind-driven waves to aerate the water. At some point, oxygen may become so depleted that it is difficult for fish to find the energy to move around. They just don't have the "wind." Additionally, the water may have cooled—perhaps another ten degrees—which slows down their piscine metabolism.

Conditions may become so inhospitable that fish become lethargic and stop eating. You can be on the ice all day and not see a flag. If jigging, you can drill a hundred holes and never get a fish. If you happen to put a lure or minnow right in front of a fish, it may tepidly strike. Otherwise, they may not be moving around enough to locate bait that has been placed even a relatively short distance away.

If a lake doesn't produce right after it ices over, it may indicate that the fishery is not in good shape. However, if a lake has been producing and then suddenly the action stops in midseason, it is time to fish elsewhere. That lake has almost surely turned off due to oxygen depletion and colder water.

The deeper areas become deoxygenated first. As the winter progresses, the dead zone expands from the bottom up closer to the surface, where there may still be at least some oxygen available. If you're fishing such a lake in midseason, placing bait just under the ice may produce results. Areas near inlets may also be worth a try. If you know the location of an underwater spring, that would be phenomenal.

However, I will assert that, in general and on average, it is a waste of time to try ice fishing a lake that has turned off. Instead, I recommend fishing on deep lakes with gravel bottoms and well-documented populations of lake trout during midseason. Such lakes are rarely subject to the oxygen depletion because they contain so much water.

As the end of winter approaches, the action often improves on shallower lakes, and it is time to return. About a month before ice-out is a reasonable date to make a first try—then every week or so afterward. I have never found an exact way to predict when fish will start to move around and resume feeding.

As spring evolves, the water warms a few degrees, and the snow starts to melt. Oxygenated water begins to flow in from tributaries, especially if there is rain. The ice will begin to melt from below, and that too may put more oxygen into the water. There was plenty there just before it froze.

Finally, many warm water species begin a prespawn staging movement to the edge of more shallow water just before the ice melts. At some point, fish begin to feed again. It's a productive time to be out there.

Late in the season, for safety, you want more than a foot of ice on the lake because it has been weakened by warmer weather. What is left is not nearly as strong as it was at the beginning of the winter. However, that last week can be extraordinarily productive and very pleasant because of the warmer temperatures.

SAFETY

Safety is an important consideration at all points of the hard water season, not just as the warmth of spring weakens the ice. At the beginning, people often go out before it is thick enough. Supposedly, two inches will support a person. However, I like to wait for about eight.

The end of the season can be tricky to assess because the ice becomes weaker and weaker as the final thawing moment approaches. The same thickness is nowhere as strong as it once was. As a rule of thumb, I think you need more than sixteen inches of ice to be safe once the temperature begins to stay above freezing all day.

Also, the ice can be fine in the morning because it has refrozen a bit after a colder night. However, as the day warms, it can become unsafe while you are fishing—and you may be oblivious to the changes occurring. If there is more than a foot or so of open water between the ice and the shore, don't go out. Conditions are too unpredictable, and being on the ice is just too dangerous.

As someone who has been there and done that, let me confirm that falling through is very serious. The frigid water quickly numbs your senses and sucks out your energy—and weak ice nearby is likely to break, making it impossible to escape.

Even with stronger ice you may not be able to get a grip and pull yourself out. If you survive, it will be due to luck more than anything else. In my case, I remembered being on a pommel horse in gymnastics. Somehow, I was able to get my back to the ice, reach behind, place my palms on the edge, and push myself up and out.

(That's why I am here today writing this book!) Also, once you are back out of the ice, try to remember to roll *away* from the open water. This distributes your weight better, and there is less chance of falling through again.

Rivers are exceptionally unpredictable. The current erodes from below in ways that are difficult to detect from above, and conditions may change quickly depending on the flow. Additional current—because of winter thaws and rainstorms—can rapidly transform a safe area into one that is "anything but." Generally, rivers should not be considered as a place to go ice fishing.

Going through the ice in a vehicle is the ultimate nightmare. I simply do not take mine out on the ice because I live too far south. The ice is often not strong enough to support a car or truck. Further north, there may well be more than two feet of ice throughout the season. However, even with ice that thick, driving may still be questionable. In particular, stay away from pressure ridges and the mouths of tributary streams.

If traveling by vehicle on the ice, keep the windows open to provide a possible emergency escape. Otherwise, if the vehicle falls through, water pressure will bind the windows and doors. You will be trapped below and almost surely die.

DRESSING FOR ICE FISHING

Knowing how to dress for ice fishing is important. It is also challenging because conditions can vary greatly, depending on the severity of the weather. It is possible to be comfortable at about zero degrees if no wind is blowing. You have to wear more layers, but that isn't a problem. A temperature in the midthirties with no wind is ideal—cold enough so you have the beauty of winter but warm enough that you don't need several layers of clothing. It is rare you get to go out on such a day.

Remember, ice fishing is supposed to be fun. It is not a contest to see if you can do it under the harshest possible conditions. If the weather is bad, I recommend finding something else to do. There is a reason they broadcast pro sports during the winter months.

Another thing to remember is that the temperature is often much colder on the ice than it is on shore. Many times I have parked at a landing in balmy forty-degree temperatures—only to discover that it was closer to twenty once I got half a mile out on the ice.

If the temperature is below ten on shore and the wind is blowing hard, it's difficult to be comfortable no matter how well dressed you may be. You need a heated ice shack to even consider fishing. It's difficult to overstate the significance of wind. If it is blowing hard, that's a critical factor in deciding where to go or whether to go at all. If no shelter is available, windchill can suck the joy right out of a day.

Be aware that wind often becomes more intense later in the afternoon, creating demanding conditions quickly and unexpectedly. You need to be able to adapt by periodically adding or subtracting layers. I recommend taking a duffel bag with extra clothing out on the ice with you. The clothing needs to lend itself well to quickly removing layers or putting them on.

Moving around to drill holes, place traps, attend to flags, release fish, and rebait is surprisingly aerobic. Your body will generate a lot of heat, and you will perspire. However, most of the time you spend on the ice is sedentary. Then, your body needs more insulation to conserve heat. The combination of sedentary and aerobic activity during cold weather is one of the fundamental challenges of ice fishing.

Heavy clothing, such as wool shirts, sweaters, parkas, and wool pants are what we think about first. However, they are just part of the puzzle, one of three basic layers.

Cotton is extremely comfortable under normal conditions. However, almost anyone who has attended a basic seminar on winter survival has heard the expression "The best dressed corpses wear cotton." In cold weather, it soaks up perspiration and retains it. The wetness then sucks the heat out of your body. This is particularly true for underwear next to the skin.

Underwear is not meant to insulate. It is meant to wick water off the skin and let it move into the outer clothing. I recommend wearing synthetic briefs and T-shirts, followed by a one-piece polyester union suit. A one-piece union suit is more comfortable under several layers of clothing because it doesn't become untucked. The polyester wicks water into the outer clothing and it also provides a certain amount of insulation.

After underwear, there may be two—even three—insulating layers. Fleece is excellent for more aerobic outdoor activities. It is lightweight, yet insulates, and it allows water (and air) to pass right through it. As functional as that may be for many endeavors, its lack of wind resistance, in my opinion, makes wool a generally better fabric for ice fishing.

Wool sweaters, shirts, and pants are heavier and insulate superbly. They are breathable, and they also have substantial wind resistance. I recommend using suspenders with wool pants and would suggest a waist size about two inches larger than normal to accommodate the layers of heavy clothing underneath.

Finally, the outer layer—the shell—is meant to shield you from the wind and preserve the heat that the insulating layers are keeping near your body. Typically, the shell material is bonded to some kind of insulation. The shell needs to be one or two sizes larger than normal in order to fit over all the heavy clothes you are wearing underneath.

Shell garments made from lightweight, high-tech fabrics are now on the market, and they are amazing. You barely feel them, but they are completely windproof and breathable. At present, however, they are still quite expensive.

I often use a shell of cotton with a little insulation built in. Such garments are durable and easy to wash. They are breathable, and they won't melt if you are around an open fire. If you are traveling by snowmobile to your ice fishing site, then by all means spend the money and buy a good snowmobile suit—ditto, a good helmet.

I recommend packing an extra sweater, plus shell layers for both your legs and upper body, in a zippered duffel bag. I like a one-piece coverall with a hood as my shell layer, as I find it takes up less space. Many people prefer a two-piece shell—a parka and overalls. They like the flexibility this offers for adjusting layers on the ice and when going in and out of a heated ice shack.

Typically, I wait until I am out on the ice and finished with the initial, more active, set of activities before I put on my shell and an extra layer of insulation. Depending on conditions, it sometimes makes more sense to put everything on before heading out on the ice.

Waterproof boots are essential. For really cold weather, I haven't found an alternative to heavy (expensive) pack boots with an insulating liner and heavy wool socks. Any boot should be at least one size larger than your normal footwear to accommodate the heavy sock—especially with the tendency for stated sizes to run a little small.

Recently, I have converted to using NEOS fabric overboots. I wear them over winter sneakers and wool socks (always with a wicking liner sock). If the temperature is above about fifteen degrees, I think this footwear is more functional because it is much lighter. Weight is no small thing. By the end of the day, you may well have walked several miles out on the ice.

You can also wear winter sneakers while traveling by vehicle to the fishing area, which makes dressing for the ice a little simpler when you reach your destination.

You should have grippers (spikes) for your boots packed in your duffel. Even a simple four-point gripper provides decent traction. Usually, if there is a little snow on the ice or the surface is rough, you don't need to worry about slipping and falling.

However, from time to time, you will encounter glare ice. The lake will be "coke-bottled up," as I like to say. Then, grippers are a godsend because—news flash—falling down on the ice is not fun. You will come down hard, most of the time, and it will hurt.

Often you see people wearing heavy mittens, which they simply remove when baiting hooks and handling fish. That works if the weather is not too cold. However, exposing your bare fingers to water under frigid conditions can be quite painful.

I think a better system is to use a tight, stretchy pair of polypropylene liner gloves underneath leather mittens. The liner gloves provide enough dexterity to bait hooks and release fish and yet still keep your fingers warm for a brief period of time. Bring an extra pair. The originals may get wet as the day progresses.

An ice fishing hat should have good wool or fleece insulation, plus a windproof shell and visor. The visor gives an angler at least some respite, as the sun can be an issue out on the ice. Similarly, high-quality, polarized, reflective sunglasses are important. Because of the cold, people don't think of the glare of bright sunlight reflecting off the snow. However, it can be intense—almost blinding.

Applying sun block and lip balm before going out on the ice is another subtle but useful practice. As counterintuitive as it may seem, it is easy to get sunburned in the winter. The sunblock also provides limited protection to your skin from cold wind.

You need to take care when exposing the raw skin of your cheeks and chin to wind chill in frigid weather. It can quickly lead to frostbite. A parka with a snorkel-type hood that you can zip up to cover your cheeks and chin is virtually essential. Often that is all that you need to protect them.

A neoprene facemask is another level of protection. It's not something people often think of, but I recommend including one with the extra clothing in your duffel bag. They really do a great job if you encounter harsh conditions.

It takes a fair amount of experimentation to develop a clothing system that you like—one that fits the type of ice fishing you do and is relatively compact. However, it's well worth the trouble. Without meaning to pontificate on the obvious, being comfortable makes the whole experience a lot better.

NUTRITION FOR ICE FISHING

Years ago, on a canoe trip in northern Canada, things did not go as planned. We ran out of food on the eleventh (and final) day of what was supposed to be an eight-day trip. We ate a meager breakfast consisting of approximately a half cup of granola apiece and began to paddle. In that debilitated condition—we capsized in a large rapid, which took what little energy we had right out of us. A few hours later, we reached the end of our journey at a boat landing in a remote Cree village. It was about forty degrees Fahrenheit with a cold, drizzling rain—miserable conditions.

We were hungry and exhausted as we pulled our canoes to shore. We knew we were going to survive. A van was due to pick us up in a few hours to take us to a restaurant. However, at that moment, four starving, skinny white people were standing in the cold—shivering and shaking—in near-freezing, wet weather.

A large Cree dressed in only a sweatshirt—but appearing totally comfortable—came over. The first words he spoke to us were, "Do you know what your problem is?" We looked at him in disbelief. "Fat," he said. "Not enough fat." Then he proceeded to tell us how important fat was in the northern climate.

We didn't say, "No shit, Dick Tracy." He was trying to be helpful. (Plus, he was as big as an offensive lineman in pro football. We didn't want to antagonize him.) We were too disoriented to explain why we hadn't been eating fat, and, of course, he had no way of knowing. Suffice it to say, a few hours later we were woofing down bacon cheeseburgers and fries.

Being outdoors in cold weather takes a *lot* of calories. Fat provides more per unit of weight than carbohydrates or protein. You almost can't get enough of it.

Proper clothing will do a lot to conserve body heat and keep you warm on the ice. However, your body needs to be properly nourished and hydrated in order to generate internal heat.

To support your body while ice fishing, you may need to double the calories you would normally consume. (I always eat a good breakfast with extra bacon or sausage on the day of the trip.) Always try to get in a substantial meal before going out on the ice. Sometimes that is breakfast; sometimes it may be lunch.

Even when you practically stagger out to the fishing grounds because of overeating, an hour later, there's a good chance you will feel hungry. Certainly, after a couple hours you should eat again. I usually pack a meat and cheese sandwich with an apple in a hard plastic container. Similarly, a small, highly insulated thermos filled with macaroni, cheese, bacon, and a dash of maple syrup is a great nutritional boost out on the ice.

Being comfortable also requires a lot of water. Because many parts of ice fishing are aerobic, you can expect to perspire like crazy. There's nothing like water to keep your body hydrated, balanced, and energized. On serious ice fishing trips—usually ones I take by myself—I go through about eight ounces per hour. There's no doubt that you feel less tired at the end of the day if you discipline yourself to stay hydrated.

A certain subset of readers is likely smirking. They are thinking about another beverage commonly used to fight dehydration on the ice. Well, yes, that's an option. If you go that route, let me recommend bottles instead of cans. The cans have a tendency to freeze to your lips if you're not careful. Also, you should know that there is no better way to trigger a flag when the action is slow than to open a beer and take that first swallow—especially if you are right in the middle of a good conversation.

Seriously, you don't want to get carried away while drinking beer out on the ice. At a minimum, you won't feel good the next morning. And, God forbid, if you get drunk in frigid weather, bad judgment can set in with catastrophic results—ranging from frostbite to life-threatening accidents. If you are on a serious, as opposed to a primarily social trip, water is a much better alternative.

GEAR AND EQUIPMENT

On that first excursion, my friend from work took me to a sporting goods store and showed me what I needed. I was pleasantly surprised by how easy it was to get started. He showed me a scoop to clear ice out of the hole, a minnow bucket, and tip-ups. Later, I acquired a power auger and a plastic sled.

I recommend Polar traps (as seen in this picture). They are simple to operate and nearly indestructible. That simplicity is a godsend if you are trying to set up when the weather is inclement—as in below zero with a howling wind. I also recommend plastic traps, in general. They are not as aesthetic, but they are lighter, easier to transport, and more durable than comparable wooden traps.

Although most anglers use tip-ups, jigging with tiny rods and small jigs tipped with plastic bait is also an effective way to ice fish. A flasher is needed to make the system work well. A flasher sends sonar signals to the bottom and displays fish as bands of light on a depth scale. Often, this enables an ice angler to see where fish are located in the water column.

For the most part, people use minnows for bait and take them on the ice in a standard bucket. You need a small net to take the minnows out. It is important to encase the inner compartment with a plastic bag to keep the water from sloshing around and bruising the little fish. You also need to make sure the bait shop fills the water right up to the brim of the bucket.

You want to securely close the plastic bag with a clamp or tie to keep water from unexpectedly spilling out during transit. Inevitably, it seems, the bucket gets turned on its side as you truck it around on the ice or in a vehicle.

A serviceable bucket can be rigged from a small cooler and two, large ziplock plastic bags (two-quart or two-and-a-half-quart sizes). This setup can take a lot of banging around when both bags are sealed. Most people use a standard bucket because it is a little easier to access bait. However, the cooler is more functional if you are using a sled or toboggan for transporting longer distances.

Once—in a moment of near total incompetence—I placed a small cooler loaded with minnows too close to the top of a pile of gear in the back of my truck. It came loose at 40 mph and took a series of nasty bounces on the pavement.

Not feeling exactly like Einstein's clone, I pulled my vehicle to the side of the road and walked back to retrieve the cooler. Imagine my amazement when I opened it to see the minnows still swimming around inside the sealed ziplock bags, unharmed by their high-speed tumble. At least, I proved to myself that the cooler and ziplock bag system worked well.

Once you get your gear and bait to the fishing grounds, you need to drill holes in the ice. When I was getting started, a clerk in a sporting goods store advised that a hand auger is fine for less than a foot of ice but suggested that it would be too much work for anything thicker than that. Then, a power auger would be best. After experimenting with hand augers, I came to believe that the clerk's opinion was correct. They are lightweight and convenient but too difficult to use on even modestly thick ice.

So I bought a power auger. These will drill through a lot of ice without much effort. However, they are heavy; and it's a lot of work to lug them around. In addition, the gas and exhaust make them dirty to handle—and the smell of gas on your hands is not exactly a fish attractant if the odor gets transferred onto your bait. Finally, they require regular maintenance if you want them to start easily under cold conditions.

More recently, I discovered the Nils Master hand auger—a relatively new design from Finland, where ice fishing is popular. It solves many of the problems associated with hand augers by using an angled pair of blades rather than flat blades—plus the crank seems to be more ergonomically efficient.

There is a six-inch model and an eight-inch model. Either will cut through two feet of ice almost as quickly as a power auger. The six-inch model is particularly efficient. Its light weight and absence of gassy smell more than compensate for the small amount of extra physical effort that is needed to drill.

A six-inch auger will drill a hole large enough to accommodate the vast majority of fish. The following bass is a fine specimen and it came through a six-inch hole with no problem.

If you anticipate catching fish larger than about three pounds, an eight-inch auger would be advisable. They do make ten-inch power augers, but I think the larger diameter would only be necessary under extraordinary fishing conditions—where you might be catching fish that weigh over ten pounds.

Ice fishing requires a lot of gear: chairs, extra clothes, food, and beverages—plus tip-ups, augers, flashers, and a jigging rod. You need a system to organize and transport it all.

I have seen people put everything in a pack basket, place it on their backs, and walk on the ice to the fishing grounds, carrying a bait bucket and/or auger. That system works well if you don't have too much stuff and aren't going very far. Pack baskets are both functional and aesthetic.

If you are traveling a ways and have a lot of gear, a toboggan or sled works much better. I have met people on the ice who were using a combination of pack baskets, wanigans (wooden boxes), and wooden toboggans. That system is a classic, nostalgic way to ice fish, and it works as well today as it did fifty years ago.

After a fair amount of experimentation, I arrived at a modern version of the same system. After much searching, I found a rugged plastic toboggan that was six feet long, a foot and a half wide, and about eight inches deep. Instead of wanigans, I decided to use a large plastic toolbox and duffel bags secured by bungee cords. The end result lacks that old-time look but is more functional. Yet, the system is very similar—really an update—to the wooden toboggans in use fifty years ago.

Shorter plastic sleds are also available, which are easier to put in the back of your vehicle. However, the shorter length makes them more difficult to pull if there is snow on the ice.

Lastly, you need a system to keep tip-ups and accessories organized and handy. By accessories, I mean sounders, pliers, extra hooks, and ice fishing rods. Pack baskets are commonly used, also the ubiquitous five-gallon plastic bucket. I think people fail to appreciate how functional a simple plastic bucket is for ice fishing.

After a lot of experimentation, I settled on a large plastic toolbox, seated in a sled. This setup does a great job of keeping everything handy. It is especially helpful right after you pull in a fish and need pliers to disgorge a hook—or a knife to cut and replace it—and then the minnow bucket to rebait. A small waist-pack with a few plastic boxes also does a great job of keeping miscellaneous gear—like extra hooks, a sounder, nail clippers, a small knife, and marker bobbers—organized and available.

However, a sled—complete with bait bucket and toolbox filled with accessories in the upper tray—is more efficient—if you manage to remember to haul everything over to the flag with you. With the top of the toolbox open—it is like having a workbench available as you remove hooks, rebait, and take pictures.

I routinely haul my gear for a mile or more. It is easy enough to do with this type of sled, especially if there is not too much snow. However, even if you have made an effort to economize on weight, there is a limit to how far you can haul gear by hand.

Commonly, wind keeps the ice fairly clear, and it is easy to walk around. However, it gets more challenging from time to time—like when the ice is covered by a layer of slush under a foot and a half of snow. Those are miserable conditions for a nonmechanized system, such as mine. The deep snow makes it difficult to haul a sled and hard to use a hand auger, especially if the slush below is thick.

With a snowmobile, those issues go away. It's no problem to haul gear, including a power auger, which will plunge right through both the ice and the top layer of slush and snow. Furthermore, with a snowmobile you can travel miles across a big lake to visit interesting areas you have identified on a depth map—and you can travel to lakes that don't have road access.

A snowmobile is a big step forward in terms of opening up opportunities for exploring new places, but it's also a big step up in terms of complexity and expense. It requires a lot of specialized equipment and clothing. Much like buying a boat, a snowmobile radically expands the options you have, and—like a boat—you will need to spend several thousand dollars to get properly equipped.

FISH—AND HOW TO FIND THEM UNDER THE ICE

If fish are not biting because the oxygen in the water under the ice has become depleted, you are unlikely to catch fish. It doesn't matter whether you are on a good spot or not. However, if the bite is on, location matters a great deal. A bathymetric (depth) map is a useful guide for identifying promising areas to jig or set tip-ups. Today, in most states, such maps are available online. Just enter the name and location of the lake into a search engine, and chances are excellent that something useful and printable will come right up.

It is commonly accepted that fish reside in relatively deeper water and then move into more shallow water to feed. They may also hold (pause) at an interim point, waiting to either move in to feed or head for deeper water to rest.

Depth maps provide a way to identify places where littoral areas (ten feet of water or less) may be connected to deeper water by a drop-off, saddle, or peninsula. Fish use these contours as paths to travel back and forth. The action can be fast and furious, if you find a good place on the underwater piscine highway.

Water is heaviest at 39.4 degrees. Therefore, water of that temperature will sink to the bottom. During the winter, colder water will be on top—in fact, close to the ice; the temperature may be just a little above freezing. At twenty feet or more, the water tends to be a few degrees warmer. If oxygen is present, the slightly warmer water seems to be more comfortable for resting fish. I have had excellent results fishing for panfish in about twenty feet, right on the bottom.

From time to time, you will encounter fish that are suspended in the middle of the water column. My theory is that they are finding the best balance they can between temperature and available oxygen. They will usually bite if a jig or minnow is presented to them at the point in water column where they are suspended.

In lakes with primarily warm water fisheries, you want to look for large littoral areas—water that is about ten feet deep, a little more or a little less. The transitional area from deeper to littoral is often more productive than the feeding area itself, possibly because the fish become more spread out once they enter it and begin to move around in search of prey.

Sometimes, but not always, the deeper basins can be good places themselves for panfish such as yellow perch, which assemble into large schools during the winter. These schools can be difficult to find, but if you do, you will be able to bring fish after fish onto the ice, one right after another.

In oligotrophic (deep, gravel bottomed) lakes, the principle of "deep water adjacent to relatively shallow" also works—in particular, for lake trout. If a depth map shows an area where water that is thirty to fifty feet deep is next to water that is one hundred feet deep, it's almost always worth trying.

As useful as depth maps may be for identifying potential places for fishing, there are limits. Many spots are productive for reasons that go beyond what a depth map can display. Such areas are usually discovered by happenstance and passed on by word of mouth.

For example, there is a great place for trout on a lake near my home, well away from any contours. The depth makes a slow transition from about four feet near the shore to ten feet about two hundred yards out. A small creek enters nearby, and that is the only possible clue. As it turns out a reef of small rocks—perhaps an acre in size—is underneath. They are just the right habitat for a species of snail, and trout actively feed on them during the winter. It is a great place to fish. However, it is not detectible through evaluating changes in depth.

Although maps are not a perfect and complete system for identifying fish-holding areas, the spots identified do work, most of the time. The examples I present in the following pages are not merely illustrations—they are actual lakes where I have caught fish. They are places that conform to a logical analysis of a bathymetric map, but they have also produced for me.

LAKE A—LITTORAL

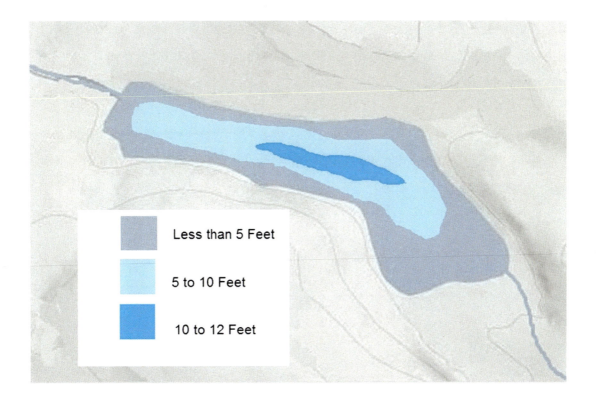

There's no better place to go right after a lake ices over than Lake A—or one with similar characteristics. This lake is about seventy acres in size, almost all of which is less than ten feet deep—except for a sliver of a basin that is just slightly more.

Lake A—and those like it—can be amazing right after ice in. Seventy acres is enough to support decent-sized fish, and you never know what you are going to get. You may get a good northern pike, walleye, or bass. You may also get trout or panfish, such as crappie or perch, depending on where you live and what species are normally available.

However, because of the shallow depth, ponds like this are quickly affected when the ice keeps the wind from recirculating and reoxygenating the water. The action normally stops a few weeks after the pond ices over. In severe winters, fish may die because there is no oxygen, and the water gets to near-freezing temperatures all the way to the bottom. Then, it may take years for the fishery to recover.

When a lake like this is good, it can be great. Although fish can be found anywhere in its waters, the slightly deeper area is by far the most productive. I've had good results in this type of lake where the deepest area was only eight feet.

LAKE B—SINGLE BASIN

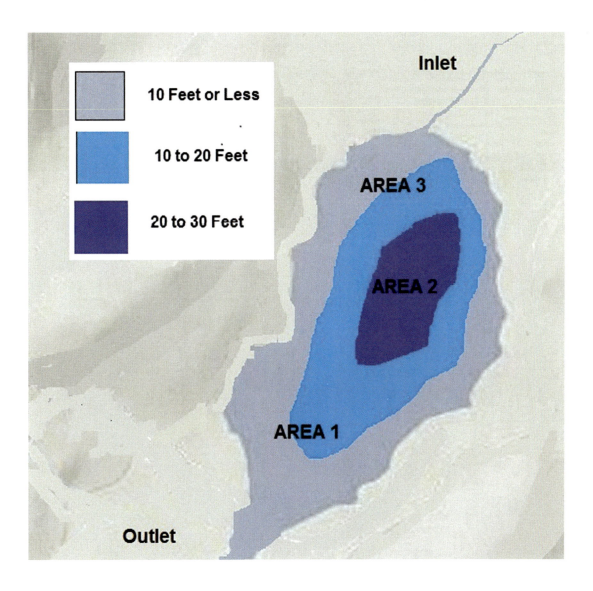

Single-basin lakes are common. Lake B is a good example. It is small, at just fifty acres. However, ponds like this can have robust fish populations. Plus, an angler can check out the whole body of water on one trip.

In smaller, shallow lakes such as Lake B, the water usually is deoxygenated below about thirty feet. However, at twenty feet it may be fine. I have experienced amazing jigging action for yellow perch on Lake B at about that depth.

I have had good results in areas 1, 2, and 3. However, the third area is the best on average. I speculate that is because an inlet brings oxygenated water into a littoral area that is adjacent to deeper water. This nice pickerel in the photo below was caught there. Incidentally, an eastern chain pickerel is an exceptionally good fish to eat, much tastier than its larger cousin, the northern pike.

LAKE C—OLIGOTROPHIC LAKE WITH A SINGLE BASIN

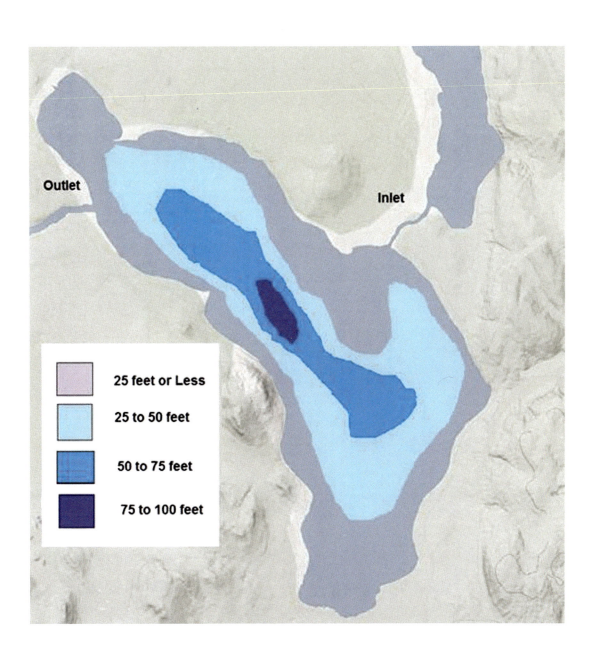

The single basin can be a productive pattern on larger oligotrophic lakes. Lake C, at a little over eight thousand acres, is a good example.

On one fishing excursion to the lake, my friend and I set our traps over the basin of deepest water. We caught this landlocked salmon and also—oddly enough—a yellow perch weighing about a pound. Our baits were placed about a foot under the ice.

Additionally, the shallow water near the inlet and outlet would be good places for brook trout. (By shallow I mean between two and four feet, not including the ice.) But be careful drilling holes in shallow water—if you put your auger into the bottom below, chances are the bits will be ruined.

LAKE D—DOUBLE BASIN AND SADDLE

Lake D is small—about sixty acres—but has two basins connected by a saddle. The little peninsula on this map practically has a flashing neon sign saying, "FISH HERE!" Both the basins and the saddle itself can be productive, and because of its small size, you can check virtually all of the lake's potentially productive areas during the course of a single afternoon.

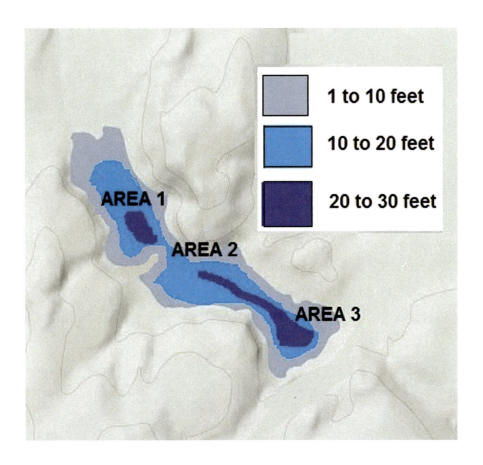

With its two deeper basins, Lake D is not as vulnerable to turning off early in the season. It's a great warm water fishery.

Yellow perch in the winter are an exceptionally good-eating fish. Once, on Lake D, I drilled a hole every one hundred feet and jigged with a flasher, starting in the basin of area 3. It took about a dozen holes to reach the edge of area 2, where a basin about twenty feet deep made a transition into the more shallow saddle area.

There, I encountered a large school of yellow perch (shown in this picture). I could have caught many more, but I disengaged after bringing about ten servings of perch to the ice. I have found this pattern to repeat in small pond after small pond.

LAKE E—SADDLES AND DROP-OFFS

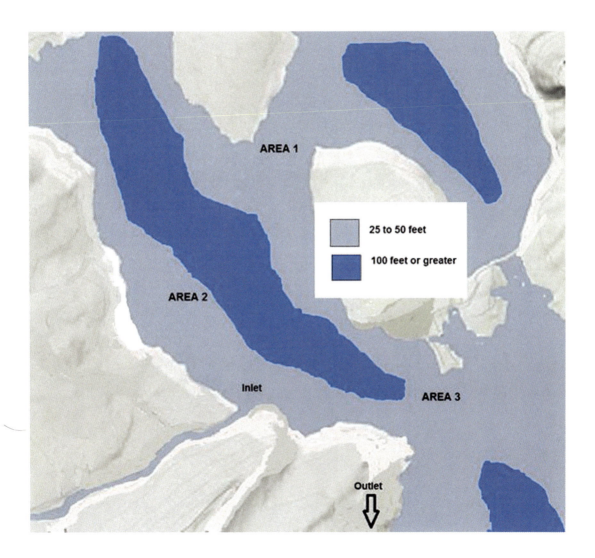

Oligotrophic Lake E is something of a factory for lake trout or "togue," as we call them in Maine. That term goes back centuries. It seems to be a Maliseet (native) word for "lake trout" that worked its way into the regional vernacular.

I simplified the legend because Lake E goes quickly from depths of thirty to fifty feet to over one hundred feet. There is so little transition that only two colors were necessary to illustrate the drop-off.

I have had good results in all three spots. Areas 1 and 3 are classic saddles. I advise setting at least one trap just below the ice over the deeper water. Then, set a line of traps across the saddle toward the other basin with the bait a foot off the bottom. Jigging from a basin across the saddle to the next basin may be productive. It is substantially more work to drill many, many holes, but usually jigging will put more fish on the ice.

Area 2 is a simple drop-off. It is the site of my very first ice fishing trip. My hosts had fished there all their lives. We did well at that location on several trips. Over the years, I've made about a dozen trips to this part of Lake E. Area 2 actually seems a little more productive than area 1—although I can see no clear reason on the map as to why that should be so.

Area 3 is likely the best spot on the entire lake, which is over thirty miles long. Area 3, at the lake's narrowest point, is located between the inlet and the outlet. Fish on the move are more likely to go through here than anywhere else.

LAKE F—UNDERWATER PENINSULAS

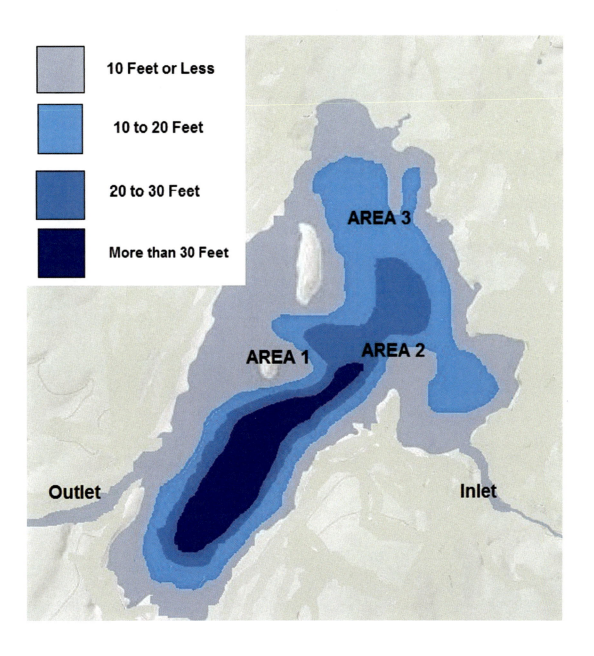

The underwater peninsula is the last feature I'd like to present. These are powerful connectors between basins and the littoral areas. They are often holding areas for fish in transit.

Lake F is about 1,200 acres. Areas 1, 2, and 3 are all productive. The contours on the map show why. Each peninsula is located near a substantial littoral area.

I have lived on Lake F for twenty-five years, and I have found area 2 to be the best. A drop-off, leading to the deepest water in the lake, is on one side; a bay, where the lake's major inlet enters, is on the other. When the bite is on, it is hard to beat. When a flag flies, it could be many kinds of fish. On one great trip, I caught the following bass and stocked brown trout from the same hole within ten minutes of each other.

Mr. Bass

Mr. Brown Trout

On another day, I went out onto the ice and discovered that parties were already set up in areas 1 and 2. So, more or less by necessity, I set up in area 3. What a discovery! To my pleasant surprise, I had very good results, catching a largemouth bass, a stocked brook trout, a white perch, a crappie, and numerous small yellow perch.

Mr. Crappie

Surprisingly, I seem to be one of the few people who knows what a good place it is. I have it pretty much to myself during a typical winter. That little peninsula doesn't look like much, but I speculate that it is a holding point on the route between deeper water and the large shallow bay to the left. There are likely positive things about area 3 that go beyond what a depth map may display.

Area 3 also confirms the importance of trial and error. Although it may seem counterintuitive when you consider all the decades that many lakes have been fished—even now, not all the good spots are known.

Depth maps provide good ideas, but the truth is in the test. Over the years, however, I have been surprised by how often maps correctly identify fish holding areas.

FISHING WITH TIP-UPS

Most ice anglers use tip-ups. They are a simple—yet deceptively sublime—method of fishing. It is primitive and intriguing to set the hook and bring the fish onto the ice—pulling the line in by hand, rather than using a rod and reel. States typically permit an ice angler to use about five traps, sometimes a few more, sometimes a few less.

Modern traps have reels underwater so the line doesn't freeze. When a fish takes the bait and pulls, the reel turns. That trips a release and sends a flag into the air. Then the fun begins.

Under frigid conditions, rebaiting and resetting a trap can be more problematic than you might think, so you want a simple design. If you are fishing in deep snow, it is best to use a model with a large, tall flag, which is easier to see.

Generally, a reel holding two hundred feet of line is adequate. However, a five-pound fish can strip one hundred feet just like that. If the reel is stripped, it is hard to predict what will happen. The fish may stop, or it may pull the reel off the trap. You just don't know. If you are targeting big fish in deep water, using a reel with a five-hundred-foot capacity is worth considering.

Line made especially for tip-ups is on the market. Generally, it is made of braided nylon or Dacron, and it seems to be all but indestructible. I put line made of Teflon-coated, braided nylon on my tip-ups many, many years ago and it still works fine. For most ice fishing, twenty-pound test line is all you will ever need. Although most tip-ups have little holes to secure your hook during storage and transport, I have found that having a few rubber bands available comes in handy for securing hooks to the reel and to the rest of the trap.

After a hole has been drilled, ice must be cleared. A lot of clearing can be accomplished by plunging the auger up and down or running the motor briefly if using a power auger. The final cleanup requires a scoop. I take two with me. If there is a lot of snow, a rugged metal scoop does the trick. To some extent, it doubles as a shovel. A smaller scoop usually does a better job of clearing ice from the hole, and I typically use my smaller scoop the most.

Usually, you want to set your traps in a line with a slight "V" facing away from the sun. That's where you sit and observe. Most of the time, it is best to drill holes about a hundred feet apart. The middle trap should be at the point of the "V" so that you will have a good view of all traps whether you are sitting in a chair or looking out from the window of an ice shack.

I recommend setting the V so that you are covering a specific area—the lip of a drop off, for example, or the edges and tip of an underwater peninsula. Although I recommend setting traps about one hundred feet apart initially, if you get a second flag on the same trap, I suggest moving another closer—drilling a hole about ten feet away.

You also need to decide where to put the bait in the water column. As counter-intuitive as it may seem, a good placement is about a foot underneath the ice. Fish often cruise just below it, regardless of the depth.

In water that is less than roughly ten feet, fish on the bottom will see the bait and swim up to get it. However, beyond that they are not as inclined to come up to investigate or strike. In deeper water, the other optimal place to set a minnow is about a foot off the bottom. Fish often hang right on the bottom.

Even if working with deeper water, I recommend setting at least one tip-up right under the ice. Placing the bait about a foot below exposes it to the most active fish in the area.

In oligotrophic lakes, large schools of smelt cruise right under ice that is over deep water. I've witnessed this personally, watching an LCD fish finder while sitting in an ice shack. About once an hour, I watched huge schools of smelt cruise below. They would pass by in a few minutes and then be gone. Bigger fish feed on these schools, which is the reason for keeping at least one trap set right under the ice on oligotrophic lakes.

Minnows are standard as bait. I prefer putting the hook through both lips, because it is easy to do and arguably places the least stress on the bait. There's also a good case to be made for putting the hook through the flesh behind the dorsal fin. Locating the point of the hook near the middle of the bait may facilitate setting the hook on a smaller fish.

Often, a fish will take the bait and run for a considerable distance before it stops and swallows. It is common practice to let the fish run and stop prior to setting the hook with a gentle tug on the line. There's no need to really put your arm into it.

Because I usually practice catch and release, I prefer to set the hook while the fish is running in order to avoid occasional gut hooking. You simply hold the line and let the fish's momentum set the hook. Most of the time, it will penetrate the fish's lip, rather than hook deeper.

Once you have the hook set, it is important to play the fish gently. There is no rod to serve as a shock absorber or a reel with a drag. A decent-sized fish can exert enough force to pull the hook—and possibly a piece of its mouth—right out. Let the line slip through your hands, applying a little resistance. After a while the fish will tire and can be brought through the hole easily enough.

If you want to release a deeply hooked fish, the best thing to do is to cut the line as near the hook as you reasonably can. That hook will eventually rust out. It is less damaging to leave it than to try to disgorge it from the gullet. If the hook is in the lip, then a pair of needle nosed pliers is ideal for removing.

I recommend using a swivel to minimize line twist, just as in fishing with a normal rod and reel. It doesn't take much weight to take bait down. A one-sixteenth ounce worm weight slip sinker placed above the swivel is all you need. Alternately, a split shot placed below the swivel also works fine.

I always place a colored bead above and below the sinker. It is useful for keeping track of where your terminal tackle is when fishing right under the ice. It also makes the terminal tackle easier to locate when it is on the ice after you have taken a fish off and need to rebait.

Arguably, the colored bead may attract a fish's attention from a distance, lead them to investigate, and strike. However, I wouldn't want to overstate the power of a colored bead, even if it is luminescent. I think it is primarily the smell and sight of bait that attracts fish.

Ice anglers use sounders—lead weights with alligator clips—for placing their bait a set distance off the bottom. By attaching the sounder to the terminal tackle, you can quickly drop it to the bottom of the lake. You then, pull it back up the desired distance, and place a marker on the line. Now you can pull the hook back up, remove the sounder, bait up, and lower the minnow to the predetermined depth.

I use small bobbers as markers. Many people just make a slip knot in their line. I prefer the bobbers because often you forget to pull the knot clear, and it becomes entangled with other line in your reel later.

I often use my flasher to position the bait exactly one foot off the bottom. The flasher gives you a precise placement and a quick view to see if there are active fish on the bottom or suspended in the water column.

Some people advise using a long leader of monofilament or fluorocarbon. I disagree. Ice fishing with tip-ups is not finesse fishing. There's just no need to go to extreme measures. The darkness below makes a finesse presentation irrelevant.

I have watched with an underwater camera, and I needed to turn on the LED light in order to see much of anything. It is *dark* under the ice. Fish generally are not that concerned with your presence. Unless you are drag racing with snowmobiles, they may not even be aware of someone on the other side of what is essentially a thick wall.

I use snelled hooks because the loop at the top is easier to connect to the snap swivel. I also recommend using a large swivel. That makes it easier to change hooks under cold, uncomfortable conditions.

Generally, you are targeting fish that weigh more than a pound. So, I recommend a size 1 or slightly larger size 1/0 hook. I think it's easier to work with a bigger hook. That's a personal opinion. Many experienced anglers use a size 2 or 4. If you are targeting smaller fish—yellow perch or crappies, for example—then you'd want to use a much smaller hook, like a size 8, and the smallest bait you can find.

Careful thought is needed to evaluate where to place your traps on a lake, as many areas are practically fishless. However, if you find a good spot, the action can be amazing. For me, a good day is getting five to ten flags in three hours of fishing.

Active fish move significant distances. On one particularly difficult excursion, my fishing partner and I found ourselves out on the ice when conditions turned miserable—freezing drizzle driven by strong winds. We had gone out the afternoon before a storm, which is actually a good time to fish on ice or open water. Theoretically, somehow the lower air pressure makes fish more willing to feed.

This time, however, as punishment for our good intentions, the storm arrived about twelve hours earlier than predicted, and we didn't have rain gear. The drizzle froze as it hit the ice. As my fishing partner and I were discussing what we might have done in our previous lives to deserve this turn of events, suddenly—because God can be so cruel—a flag flew on our most distant trap.

Mercifully, we were in a vehicle, sitting comfortably with the engine and heater running. The weather was so bad that we drove over to attend to the tip-up. To our surprise, we found two hooks with lines in the mouth of a nice lake trout. At first, it was mystifying. However, we soon discovered that freezing rain had disabled the flag on a trap right next to where we'd been parked, maybe two hundred feet away. Nearly all the line had been stripped before that fish found another meal below that second trap.

The mobile nature of fish under the ice is the reason ice anglers commonly leave their tip-ups in the same place the entire time they are out. I disagree—even though once in a while, a trap that has lain dormant for hours will produce. Usually, if fish are around, a flag will fly within a half hour. Often, it will fly in less than five minutes.

If a trap hasn't produced within the first fifteen minutes, check the bait to make sure you are not fishing on credit. Keep checking the bait every hour or so. If there haven't been any flags within an hour, consider moving the trap at least one hundred feet. The new location may not produce either, but I will assert that at least your odds are a little better.

Fishing with tip-ups is highly social. You and your friends go to a generally promising area, set up traps all over the place, and then relax. If the weather is decent, break out the lawn chairs. If not, fire up the stove in the ice shack.

There never seems to be a shortage of fun things to talk about while waiting for flags to fly: past fishing trips, future fishing trips, sex, drugs, rock and roll music, politics, sports, professional wrestling—whatever. It is also rumored that ice anglers enjoy an occasional beer while visiting with their friends, waiting for fish to bite.

JIGGING

With tip-ups, you are using time to test an area. If active fish are in the vicinity, sooner or later they will swim close enough to find the bait and strike.

With jigging, you are using mobility to test a much larger area. When jigging, I usually cover well over a mile. I typically test between twenty and thirty holes. Hard-core jiggers do way more than that. Often, it is well worth the effort because, if you locate active fish, sometimes there are a *lot* of them.

For jigging, the Nils Master hand auger is fine if the ice is less than about a foot and a half thick. If the ice is thicker, a hand auger becomes questionable because of the sheer number of holes you need to drill. With a power auger, a pair of anglers working together can "Swiss cheese" an area without much effort. Then, they just jig from hole to hole. On solo trips, I typically drill about five holes a hundred feet apart. I leave the power auger at the last hole and go back to my gear. I jig the holes until I reach the auger—and then repeat.

Jigging is a more active method of ice fishing. Success is related to the sheer number of holes you test and the logic you are using to choose an area. It can be done in a group, but it is often a solitary pursuit. Also, it is more technical due to the ideas you may be using to locate fish.

It is possible to jig without electronics and a shelter. You slowly lower the jig to the bottom. Then, raise it a foot or so. If fish are active, they will quickly strike.

Serious jiggers use sonar flashers and flip-style shelters that set up almost instantly. A seat is built into a plastic shed with hoops attached to a fabric tent. All the angler needs to do is flip the hoops forward to establish a decent, windproof shelter and place themselves in a comfortable position to fish.

Usually, you are working with a smaller jig, no more than one-sixteenth ounce, tipped with a live minnow or plastic. I've had good luck with Berkley Gulp! in the maggot or inch-and-a-half minnow size.

Use jig designs that lend themselves to a horizontal presentation. Generally, the length of the jig should be parallel to the bottom. The eyelet should be near the center of the jig. They should be painted with luminescent paint. If you are targeting big fish such as walleye, northern pike, or large lake trout, a bigger lure is appropriate. However, I have caught many three-pound bass on tiny jigs tipped with Gulp!.

If no immediate action develops, it's a good idea to beat the jig up and down on the bottom in an effort to attract some piscine attention. Then, raise it about a foot and subtly twitch it. If you still are not getting any action, by far the best bet is to move. If active fish are present, they will strike almost immediately. In my experience, a minute to test a hole is usually forty-five seconds too long.

If you are jigging in a good spot, the flasher may display fish suspended in the water column or resting just a few inches off the bottom. It's common for them to rest right on the bottom itself, and when they do, you can't see them—even with the flasher. However, as your jig approaches, bands of light will erupt from the bottom as they rise to strike.

Flashers enable an angler to identify and present a jig to suspended fish. That is an important advantage, which almost by itself justifies purchasing a flasher. If you've never used a flasher on the ice, I recommend going to YouTube and entering "ice fishing with sonar flashers" in the search box. Many excellent videos will appear to guide you through the process. It is quite simple once you become familiar.

Strikes in cold water are subtle. That's why very lightweight equipment is used. The tip of a short, ultralight pole may only bend half an inch if a fish has bitten. That's all you need to see—set the hook and start reeling.

Many anglers use micro light spinning reels spooled with either two- or four-pound test line, specifically formulated for ice fishing. I've had very good results with such an outfit. However, a spinning reel tends to put a coil in the line. Even with a tiny swivel a foot or so up from the jig, it will spin around like crazy for a while. Every time you reel up, it resets the coil so when you get to the next hole there is more spin.

It doesn't look right. I know I've caught many fish with a spinning outfit, but the appearance always concerned me. The answer is a flat line reel. They look like little fly fishing reels. Spooled with a braided line formulated for ice fishing, they work well. You put the line on by reeling backward, just like a fly reel.

The presentation looks more natural. There is minimal twirling to the jig. With a flasher, lower the jig by reeling forward until you have it where you want in the water column. It's more efficient, in my opinion, than opening the bail on a spinning reel and letting the lure drop.

If you are using electronics, when you happen across a big school of fish, the display can be amazing to watch—less so, if there is just one on the prowl. However, even then, the sight of a red band of light moving off the bottom and nailing your jig is fascinating to watch.

For panfish, I recommend two-pound line, specially formulated for ice fishing. Four-pound test is adequate for most other situations. If you are fortunate enough to be targeting really big fish, then, obviously, heavier tackle is needed.

Although it is possible to jig without electronics and a portable jigging shelter such as the Clam Fish Trap, I think it is well worth spending the money to purchase a hooped shelter and flasher.

ICE SHELTERS

Often, despite wearing several layers of clothing, it is too cold to be comfortable sitting in a chair on the ice. In those cases, it's time to think about the next level of protection. Similarly, if it is too cold to be comfortable jigging in a flip-up shelter, then it is time to consider jigging through a hole in the floor of something more heavy duty.

There are many portable shelters on the market today. Designs have evolved and improved noticeably over the years. However, "portable" is a term that requires a certain amount of qualification. Almost any shelter weighs at least thirty pounds, which means that transporting it any great distance to the fishing grounds, may not be easy. You have to think about both the shelter and the system you have available to take it out on the ice.

As of 2014, I believe that a small hub shelter is the best combination of comfort and portability. They don't have floors, so at least one person can fish inside— either with a tip-up or by jigging. Despite not having a floor, they are surprisingly windproof. With the doors zipped closed, solar gain is enough to keep them comfortable, even at low temperatures.

The creator of the hub shelter should get an award for design. The struts are internal. There is not much flat surface to act as a sail. They unfold, almost like a lawn chair. They can be easily erected or packed up in just a couple of minutes.

If the wind is blowing strong, it can collapse a hub that does not have an external anchor, so I recommend starting with one external anchor attached to the hub that is pointing into the wind and then installing internal anchors as needed. A long bungee cord works well as a line. (Anchor here refers to a large metal bolt that you screw into the ice.)

Obviously, there are limits. When Mother Nature serves up subzero temperatures and powerful winds, there's only so much designers can do to provide protection with shelters that are essentially tents.

The next step is a full-fledged, permanent, heated ice shack that you keep out on a frozen lake for a season. Building and maintaining it require considerable time and expense, and you have to use it nearly every weekend to make it worthwhile, in my opinion.

A small screw-on heater for a one-pound propane cylinder is enough to keep a well-made ice shack comfortable. However, typically, people use a twenty-pound cylinder and run a hose inside to a larger portable heater. I prefer a small woodstove as a heat source. It is more expensive to buy and install, and you need to keep a supply of wood on hand, but it is quieter and provides heat that is easier to regulate.

Using an ice shack as a base for family activity can work very well. It's a structured, relaxing place to take children. They enjoy being able to go out and run around on the ice and then come back into a warm room, eat a hot dog, and drink a cup of hot chocolate. For the most part, you don't need to worry about them getting cold.

It's hard to build a good ice shack for less than $1,000, by the time you get done with everything. Then, you need a trailer to take the shack from your residence to a lake. Once you get it there, you need to get the shack out on the ice—maybe towing the trailer with an ATV or snowmobile.

Once it is in place, you need to attend to the shack at least once a week. No matter how well you place the blocks under the runners, they have a tendency to melt into the ice, and it can be a fair amount of work to chip them free, reblock, and level the shack.

At the end of the season, you will need to recruit friends to help you take it off the ice, and you will have to find a place to store it for eight months. If renting an ice shack is an option, I think that is the best way to go. They charge a steep price for a day's rental, but, generally, it is far less expensive than owning one personally.

Fishing from an ice shack essentially trades mobility for comfort. If there is no action, you are pretty much stuck in that one place. However, if the bite is on nearby, it's great. There's almost no more pleasant way to spend a winter afternoon than sitting in comfort with friends, looking at your tip-ups through a window, and every so often leaving the luxury of that heated room to go out and haul up a fish.

CLOSING

Ice fishing bears many similarities to that observation about Texas Hold'em poker—someone can learn the basics very quickly, but a lifetime isn't long enough to master all the nuances. I have learned something new on nearly every trip. It's a pleasurable learning curve that doesn't seem to end.

There's no substitute for time on the ice, and there's also no substitute for reading books, magazine articles, and watching DVDs. In recent years, the Internet and YouTube have evolved as other high-quality sources of information. A lot of helpful material is posted by enthusiastic people who love to ice fish. It's almost always worthwhile to visit YouTube and see what may be available.

Ice fishing has been substantially expanded by anglers and writers living in the upper Midwest. In 1991, I read a book entitled *Ice Fishing Secrets* by Al Linder, Doug Stange, and Dave Genz that changed my whole approach. It is still a classic. It's hard to recommend it and a parallel DVD enough.

Doug Stange is the longtime editor of *In-Fisherman* magazine, which issues an annual guide to ice fishing. It can be hard to find on newsstands, so I usually call and order it in late November. I consider it a must read, if you want to stay familiar with new trends, tackle, and techniques. The magazine typically comes with catalogues from vendors carrying highly specialized products that are difficult to find in normal sporting goods stores.

Dave Genz was the technical advisor for another excellent book entitled *Modern Methods of Ice Fishing* by Tom Gruenwald. It too is a classic. Gruenwald has written many other worthwhile books about ice fishing. He is associated with HT Enterprises, whose founder, Paul Grahl, invented the Polar Tip-Up.

For decades, Dave Genz has been in the forefront of developing ice fishing gear and methods. He invented the original hooped shelter, the Fish Trap, and has pioneered the use of flashers. There's no such thing as a lifetime achievement award in ice fishing, but if there were Mr. Genz would be at the top of nearly everyone's nominating list.

I feel a debt of gratitude to these ice fishing pioneers. I have written this book as a long-term student. I would still be looking out the window of an ice shack at a line of tip-ups were it not for the knowledge they have shared. I wouldn't be catching nearly as many fish or having as much fun.

There are many ways to enjoy ice fishing. As with open water, it is common for people to travel long distances to remote areas in the north. Personally, I like relatively short trips close to my home in Maine. My system is geared to taking everything out onto the ice by hand in a plastic toboggan.

I've never taken the next step—purchasing a snowmobile and high-tech modern clothing. That would open up some fascinating trips! I've always had a desire to go into the bush by snowmobile or dog sled, hot camp in a wall tent with a small wood stove, and enjoy ice fishing in the context of a wilderness experience. Someday, hopefully, I will.

I am confident that the methods I have described would work just fine under more extreme conditions. I believe they are solid fundamental skills that would serve ice anglers well under most circumstances. I hope the information I provided in this book has been helpful. I wish my readers the joy of the experience and the best of success at the fascinating activity of ice fishing.

Made in the USA
Monee, IL
15 November 2020